What the Light Was Like

# AMY CLAMPITT

---

*What the Light*
*Was Like*

*faber and faber*

LONDON · BOSTON

First published in the USA in 1985
by Alfred A. Knopf Inc., New York
and simultaneously in Canada
by Random House of Canada Limited, Toronto

First published in Great Britain in 1986
by Faber and Faber Limited
3 Queen Square London WC1N 3AU
Reprinted 1987

Printed in Great Britain by
Redwood Burn Limited
Trowbridge, Wiltshire
All rights reserved

British Library Cataloguing in Publication Data

Clampitt, Amy
What the light was like.
I. Title
811'.54    PS3553.L23
ISBN  0–571–13814–4

For their help with this book, the author wishes to record her thanks to Harold Korn, Howard Moss, Doris Myers, Alice Quinn, Mallory Rintoul, Mary Jo Salter, Linda Spencer, and Helen Vendler, as well as to the John Simon Guggenheim Foundation for its support in 1982–83, when a number of the poems included here were written.


Grateful acknowledgment is made to the following periodicals, in which poems in this collection have previously appeared: *The Anglican Theological Review*, "Urn-Burial and the Butterfly Migration"; *Antaeus*, "Burial in Cypress Hills"; *Grand Street*, "A Curfew," "He Dreams of Being Warm" (under the title "Keats at Hampstead"), "High Culture," "The Isle of Wight" (under the title "Keats on the Isle of Wight"), "Losing Track of Language," "Margate" (under the title "Keats at Margate"), "Teignmouth" (under the title "Keats at Teignmouth"), "Winchester: The Autumn Equinox" (under the title "Keats at Winchester"), "Written in Water"; *The Kenyon Review*, "The Elgin Marbles" (under the title "Keats and the Elgin Marbles"), "The Reedbeds of the Hackensack"; *The Massachusetts Review*, "The Sacred Hearth Fire"; *New England Review*, "Chichester" (under the title "Keats at Chichester"), "A New Life"; *The New Republic*, "Witness"; *The New Yorker*, "The August Darks," "A Baroque Sunburst," "Black Buttercups," "Cloudberry Summer," "The Cooling Tower," "From a Clinic Waiting Room," "Low Tide at Schoodic," "The Spruce Has No Taproot," "Time," "Vacant Lot with Tumbleweed and Pigeons," "Voyages," "What the Light Was Like"; *Poetry*, "Gooseberry Fool," "The Hickory Grove," "Homer, A.D. 1982"; *Prairie Schooner*, "A Cure at Porlock," "The Godfather Returns to Color TV," "Let the Air Circulate," "Real Estate," "Ringing Doorbells," "A Scaffold," "Townhouse Interior with Cat."

"The Reedbeds of the Hackensack" also appeared in *The Pushcart Prize: The Best of the Small Presses*, VIII. The eight poems here included in the section entitled "Voyages" were published by the Sarabande Press in a limited edition as *A Homage to John Keats*.

*To the memory
of my brother Richard
1925–1981*

# CONTENTS

## V

### WRITTEN IN WATER

*Ay, on the shores of darkness there is light,*
*And precipices show untrodden green.*
                    —Keats, "To Homer"

# I

## THE SHORE

# A BAROQUE SUNBURST

struck through such a dome
as might await a groaning Michelangelo,
finding only alders and barnacles
and herring gulls at their usual squabbles,
sheds on the cove's voluted
silver the aloof skin tones
of a Crivelli angel: a region,
a weather and a point of view
as yet unsettled, save for the lighthouse
like a Venetian campanile, from whose nightlong
reflected angelus you might suppose
the coast of Maine had Europe
on the brain or in its bones, as though
it were a kind of sickness.

# THE AUGUST DARKS

Stealth of the flood tide, the moon dark
but still at work, the herring shoals
somewhere offshore, looked for
but not infallible, as the tide is,
as the August darks are—

stealth of the seep of daylight, the boats
bird-white above the inlet's altering
fish-silver, the murmur of the motor
as the first boat slips out
ahead of daylight

into the opening aorta, that heaving
reckoning whose flux informs the heart-
beat of the fisherman—poor,
dark, fallible-infallible
handful of a marvel

murmuring unasked inside the ribcage,
workplace covert as the August darks are,
as is the moon's work, masked within
the blazing atrium of daylight,
the margin of its dwindling

sanguine as with labor, but effortless:
as is the image, far out, illusory
at the dark's edge, of the cruise ship
moving, seemingly unscathed by effort,
bright as a stage set

for the miming of the tiara'd swan's danced
dying, the heartbeat's prodigies of strain
unseen, the tendons' ache, the blood-
stained toe shoes, the tulle
sweat-stained, contained

out where the herring wait, beyond
the surf-roar on the other side of silence
we should die of (George Eliot
declared) were we to hear it. Many
have already died of it.

Force, just here, rolls up
pomaded into vast blue curls
fit for the Sun King, then crumples
to a stuff of ruffs and kerchiefs
over ruined doorposts, the rubble
of an overthrow no one remembers
except through cooled
extrapolation—tunnels
underneath the granite,
the simmering moat, the darkened sill
we walk on now,
prowling the planar windowpanes of tidepools
for glimpses of kelp's ribboned whips,
the dead men's fingers.
                        Boulders
smothered in a fur of barnacles
become a slum, a barrio
of hardened wigwams, each
(notwithstanding a seeming armor
that invites, when added to the fate
of being many, the hobnails
of a murderous indifference)
holding an entity no less
perishably tender than any
neonate delivered, red
and squalling, in the singular.
                            Spruces,
turreted above the ledge,
lodge in the downdraft
of their precarious stairwells

a warbler who, all nerves tuned to
alarums, dapper in a yellow domino,
a noose of dark about his throat,
appends his anxious signature—
a wiry wheeze,
a blurred flute note.

# BERTIE GOES HUNTING

*For Mary Jo Salter and Brad Leithauser*

Dear beast, luxurious of pelt,
moon-orbed possessor of the
screen-door-unlatching paw,
the lurk that twitches in
   the haunch at every

piebald quiver of out-in-the-
open; past the fern-flanked
porchside boundary, a froth
of goldenrod and timothy
   absorbs his predatory

crouch-and-spring, quick-
silver underside of memory,
the lunge-evoking, paradisal
rustle of the underbrush, the
   just-missed quarry:

his vanishings into a history
so dense with molecules, so
chary of the traceable, you
never quite believe the ata-
   vism's only temporary—

that à la the silver lizards
Robert Frost purported to have
seen cascading down the
mountainside in slush-time,
   this time the furry

entity you knew, if not quite
yet dissolved into a dew, will
have surrendered to the texture
of that habitat, the slither
    of its understory.

Yet when you call the name you've
given him, that like a skipped
stone skims the surface of what-
ever's out there, something,
    primed to be ready for a

game of shake-and-bake, a fondling
session, with the inevitable risk
of being laughed at—is it habit,
is it altogether voluntary?—
    brings him in a hurry.

First ventured into
in mid-July, the bog's sodden hollow
muffled the uproar of the shore
it hunkered in the lee of. Wrung residues
of sphagnum moss steeped in self-
manufactured acids stained the habitat's
suffusing waters brown,

to feed the red-
haired, hair-trigger sundews' mazy glint,
the ground-level pseudo-pomegranate
drowning dens of pitcher plants. Sheer dearth,
a poverty of nitrogen, they tell us,
is what turned this vegetation predatory
as the blood-craving

blackflies and
mosquitoes it has evolved its several
macabre ways of preying on. Bog
laurel and lambkill distil a nectar and a
petty poison of their own. Rancor
is rarely simple, least so in the dank
sector of organic

chemistry. Likewise
its lack, as in these strangely sallow-
tinged, blandly baked-apple-
flavored thimble nubbins, singly borne, no
more than inches from the bog's
sour surface. Could so odd a crop
be edible? Yes,

it could. Called
hayth- (but spell it *heath*) berries by
the populace Down East, they're
known and relished as cloudberries farther north.
Here, they figure as subarctic strays—
pale-jeweled morsels of seed and sweetness
for some ravenous

small mammal to
wring a minim's undiluted, untainted
pleasure from, the distillation
of a boreal summer's luminous, perfervid,
snow-ringed haven. And a rare thing
pleasure is too, even for the mammal who
in effect invented

and then lost no
time polluting it, in ways the wretchedest
den-fouling lemming would surely
find astonishing. A thing still rarer (or so
for me it was) than that cloud-
berry summer is what in June, not quite a
summer later,

would prove on
bemused observation to be a thriving
cloudberry spring: revisited, the
bog's sunken floor a dapple of such countless,
singly borne, close-to-the-
ground corollas, each of a whiteness
so without a flaw

I thought, for
half a second, *Snow*. But no. Some new
species, then? A moonflake
guelder rose? I stooped to look. A clue
appeared: the stem beneath each
flower bore a paired leaf-clasp, its
halves consisting

of two pale,
wizened infant claws; and as the wavering
appendage of a single barnacle
is multiplied, on observation, to a kind of choir
(what are they doing? Merely
seizing any passing thing that may be
edible), thereby

tending to unhand
one's sense of balance, I swam, immersed
in undersurfaces, the filling tide-
pool of surprise. Days later—all those claws
by now mere greenery, the whiteness fallen—
the whole unstable, illusory van of pleasure
had moved on.

# GOOSEBERRY FOOL

The gooseberry's no doubt an oddity,
an outlaw or pariah even—thorny
and tart as any
kindergarten martinet, it can harbor
like a fernseed, on its leaves' under-
side, bad news for pine trees,
whereas the spruce
resists the blister rust
it's host to. That veiny Chinese
lantern, its stolid jelly
of a fruit, not only has
no aroma but is twice as tedious
as the wild strawberry's sunburst
stem-end appendage: each one must
be between-nail-snipped at both extremities.

Altogether, gooseberry virtues
take some getting
used to, much as does trepang,
tripe à la mode de Caen,
or having turned thirteen.
The acerbity of all things green
and adolescent lingers in
it—the arrogant, shrinking,
prickling-in-every-direction thorn-
iness that loves no company except its,
or anyhow that's what it gets:
bristling up through gooseberry ghetto sprawl
are braced thistles' silvery, militantly symmetrical
defense machineries. Likewise inseparably en-
tangled in the disarray of an
uncultivated childhood, where gooseberry bushes (since
rooted out) once flourished, is

the squandered volupté of lemon-
yellow-petaled roses' luscious flimflam—
an inkling of the mingling into one experience
of suave and sharp, whose supremely im-
probable and far-fetched culinary
embodiment is a gooseberry fool.

Tomorrow, having stumbled into
this trove of chief ingredients
(the other being very thickest cream)
I'll demonstrate it for you. Ever since,
four summers ago, I brought you,
a gleeful Ariel, the trophy
of a small sour handful,
I've wondered what not quite articulated thing
could render magical
the green globe of an unripe berry.
I think now it was simply
the great globe itself's too much to carry.

# THE SPRUCE HAS NO TAPROOT

Cats, as a rule, don't take to travel
any better than the lobed, immobile
lichen whose tenure in the rock's
bleak niches, though it lacks
roots, is all but fanatical.

Likewise the cinquefoil: though nebulous
of flower head and petal
as a yard of dotted Swiss,
it keeps, under the froufrou, a profile
low as any fugitive's. The strawberry's

red skeins crisscross the gravel
with such rigor you might suppose
it knew the habitat to be untenable
unless tied down. So do the rootstocks
of the rose its cousin, whose colonies

along the coast rise as they widen
into a mimic mountain.
Depth isn't everything: the spruce
has no taproot, but to hold on
spreads its underpinnings thin—

a gathering in one continuous,
meshing intimacy, the interlace
of unrelated fibers
joining hands like last survivors
who, though not even neighbors

hitherto, know in their predicament
security at best is shallow.
Whoever fancies an uprooted fragment
of the coast of Maine might settle into
a New York apartment—foolish,

unnatural whim!—discovers what
must have possessed the cat
when, rather than go through
one more uprooting, she hid out,
a fugitive fanatic who

instead preferred to starve and stiffen.
Found too late, according to her wish
what's left of her is now in-
extricable from the ground. Every
day for weeks, half a can of Figaro

flavored with liver or tunafish
waited out there for her. Every night
for weeks, some mobile opportunist
slipped in from the forest
to banquet from her dish.

# WHAT THE LIGHT WAS LIKE

*For Louise Dickinson Rich*
*and the family of Ernest Woodward*

Every year in June—up here, that's the month for lilacs—
      almost his whole front yard,
with lobster traps stacked out in back, atop the rise
      that overlooks the inlet
would be a Himalayan range of peaks of bloom,
      white or mauve-violet,

gusting a turbulence of perfume, and every year the same
      iridescent hummingbird,
or its descendant, would be at work among the mourning cloaks
      and swallowtails, its motor loud,
its burning gorget darkening at moments as though charred.
      He kept an eye out

for it, we learned one evening, as for everything that flapped
      or hopped or hovered
crepuscular under the firs: he'd heard the legendary
      trilling of the woodcock,
and watched the eiders, once rare along these coasts,
      making their comeback

so that now they're everywhere, in tribes, in families
      of aunts and cousins,
a knit-and-purl of irresistibly downy young behind them, riding
      every cove and inlet;
and yes, in answer to the question summer people always ask,
      he'd seen the puffins

that breed out on  Tit Manan, in summer improbably clown-faced
        behind the striped scarlet
of Commedia dell' Arte masks we'll never see except in
        Roger Tory Peterson's
field guide, or childish wishful thinking. There was much
        else I meant to ask about

another summer. But in June, when we came limping up here
        again, looking forward
to easing up from a mean, hard, unaccommodating winter,
        we heard how he'd gone out
at dawn, one morning in October, unmoored the dinghy
        and rowed to his boat

as usual, the harbor already chugging with half a dozen
        neighbors' revved-up craft,
wet decks stacked abaft with traps, the bait and kegs stowed
        forward, a lifting weft
of fog spooled off in pearl-pink fleeces overhead with the first
        daylight, and steered,

as usual, past first the inner and then the outer bar, where in
        whatever kind of weather,
the red reef-bell yells, in that interminable treble, *Trouble*,
        out past where the Groaner
lolls, its tempo and forte changing with the chop, played on
        by every wind shift,

straight into the sunrise, a surge of burning turning the
        whole ocean iridescent
fool's-gold over molten emerald, into the core of that
        day-after-day amazement—
a clue, one must suppose, to why lobstermen are often
        naturally gracious:

maybe, out there beside the wheel, the Baptist spire
        shrunk to a compass-
point, the town an interrupted circlet, feeble as an apron-
        string, for all the labor
it took to put it there, it's finding, out in that ungirdled
        wallowing and glitter,

finally, that what you love most is the same as what you're
        most afraid of—God,
in a word; whereas it seems they think they've got it licked
        (or used to), back there
in the Restricted Area for instance, where that huge hush-
        hush thing they say is radar

sits sprawling on the heath like Stonehenge, belittling every
        other man-made thing
in view, even the gargantuan pods of the new boat hulls you
        now and then see lying,
stark naked, crimson on the inside as a just-skinned carcass,
        in Young's boatyard,

even the gray Grange Hall, wood-heated by a yardarm of stovepipe
        across the ceiling.
Out there, from that wallowing perspective, all comparisons
        amount to nothing,
though once you've hauled your last trap, things tend to wander
        into shorter focus

as, around noon, you head back in: first 'Tit Manan lighthouse,
        a ghostly gimlet
on its ledge by day, but on clear nights expanding to a
        shout, to starboard,
the sunstruck rock pile of Cranberry Point to port; then
        you see the hamlet

rainbowed, above the blurring of the spray shield, by the
        hurrying herring gulls'
insatiable fandango of excitement—the spire first, then
        the crimson boat hulls,
the struts of the ill-natured gadget on the heath behind them
        as the face of things expands,

the hide-and-seek behind the velvet-shouldered, sparse
        tree-spined profiles,
as first the outer, then the inner bar appears, then the scree-
        beach under Crowley Island's
crowding firs and spruces, and you detect among the chimneys
        and the TV aerials,

yours. But by midafternoon of that October day,
        when all his neighbors'
boats had chugged back through the inlet, his
        was still out; at evening,
with half the town out looking, and a hard frost
        settling in among the alders,

there'd been no sign of him. The next day, and the next,
        the search went on,
and widened, joined by planes and helicopters from as
        far away as Boston.
When, on the third day, his craft was sighted
        finally, it had drifted,

with its engine running, till the last gulp of fuel
        spluttered and ran out,
beyond the town's own speckled noose of buoys, past
        the furred crest of Schoodic,
vivid in a skirt of aspens, the boglands cranberry-
        crimson at its foot,

past the bald brow the sunrise always strikes first, of
      the hulk of Cadillac,
riding the current effortlessly as eiders tied to water
      by the summer molt,
for fifty miles southwestward to where, off Matinicus,
      out past the rock

that, like 'Tit Manan, is a restricted area, off limits for
      all purposes but puffins',
they spotted him, slumped against the kegs. I find it
      tempting to imagine what,
when the blood roared, overflowing its cerebral sluiceway,
      and the iridescence

of his last perception, charring, gave way to unreversed,
      irrevocable dark,
the light out there was like, that's always shifting—from
      a nimbus gone berserk
to a single gorget, a cathedral train of blinking, or
      the fogbound shroud

that can turn anywhere into a nowhere. But it's useless.
      Among the mourning-cloak-
hovered-over lilac peaks, their whites and purples,
      when we pass his yard,
poignant to excess with fragrance, this year we haven't
      seen the hummingbird.

# II

## THE HINTERLAND

# BLACK BUTTERCUPS

In March, the farmer's month
for packing up and moving on, the rutted
mud potholed with glare, the verb *to move*
connoted nothing natural, such as the shifting
of the course of streams or of the sun's
position, sap moving up, or even
couples dancing. What the stripped root, exhumed
above the mudhole's brittle skin, discerned
was exile.

        Exile to raw clapboard,
a privy out in back, a smokehouse
built by the pioneers, no shade trees
but a huddle of red cedars, exposure
on the highest elevation in the township,
a gangling windmill harped on by each
indisposition of the weather,
the mildewed gurgle of a cistern
humped underneath it like a burial.

                Menace
inhabited that water when the pioneers,
ending their trek from North Carolina, farther
than Ur of the Chaldees had been from Canaan,
settled here and tried to root themselves:
four of the family struck down on this farm
as its first growing season ended. Menace
still waited, literally around the corner,
in the graveyard of a country church,
its back against the timber
just where the terrain began to drop (the creek
down there had for a while powered a sawmill,
but now ran free, unencumbered, useless)—
that not-to-be-avoided plot whose honed stones'
fixed stare, fanned in the night

by passing headlights, struck back
the rueful semaphore:
*There is no safety.*

                      I was ten years old.
Not three miles by the road that ran
among the farms (still less if
you could have flown, or, just as unthinkable,
struck out across country, unimpeded
by barbed wire or the mire of feedlots)
the legendary habitat of safety
lay contained: the memory
of the seedleaf in the bean, the blind
hand along the bannister, the virgin sheath
of having lived nowhere but here. Back there
in the dining room, last summer's
nine-year-old sat crying on the window seat
that looked into the garden, rain
coursing the pane in streams, the crying
on the other side and it one element—and sits
there still, still crying, knowing
for the first time forever what it was
to be heartbroken.

                    The look of exile
foreseen, however massive or inconsequential,
hurts the same; it's the remembered
particulars that differ. How is one to measure
the loss of two blue spruces, a waterfall
of bridal wreath below the porch, the bluebells
and Dutchman's-breeches my grandmother
had brought in from the timber
to bloom in the same plot with peonies
and lilies of the valley? Or, out past
the pasture where the bull, perennially

[26]

resentful, stood for the menace of authority
(no leering, no snickering in class),
an orchard—or a grove of willows
at the far edge of the wet meadow
marking the verge, the western barrier
of everything experience had verified? We never
thought of going there except in February,
when the sap first started working up
the pussywillow wands, the catkins
pink underneath a down of eldritch silver
like the new pigs whose birthing coincided,
shedding their crisp cupolas' detritus
on the debris of foundering snowbanks
brittle as the skin of standing ponds
we trod on in the meadow, a gauche travesty
of calamity like so many entertainments—
the nuptial porcelain, the heirloom crystal
vandalized by wanton overshoes, bundled-up
boredom lolling, while the blue world reeled
up past the pussywillow undersides of clouds
latticed by swigging catkins soon to haze
with pollen-bloat, a glut
run riot while the broken pond
unsealed, turned to mud
and, pullulating, came up buttercups
lucent with a mindlessness as total
as the romp that ends up wet-mittened,
chap-cheeked, fretful beside the kitchen stove,
later to roughhouse or whine its way
upstairs to bed.
                        Night froze it up again
for the ten thousandth time, closing the seals
above the breeding ground of frogs, the Acheron

of dreadful disappointed Eros
stirring up hell—the tics,
the shame, the pathological ambition,
anxiety so thick sometimes that nothing
breeds there except more anxiety,
hampering yet another generation, all
the sodden anniversaries of dread:
black buttercups that never see daylight
or with lucent chalices drink of the sun.
Did we then hear them moving
wounded from room to room? Or in what shape
was it we first perceived it—the unstanched
hereditary thing, working its way
along the hollows of the marrow,
the worry taking root within like ragweed,
the noxious pollen flowering into
nothing but sick headaches
passed down like an heirloom? When,
under the same roof the memory of
a legendary comfort had endowed
with what in retrospect would seem
like safety, did the rumor
of unhappiness arrive? I remember waking,
a February morning leprous with frost
above the dregs of a halfhearted snowfall,
to find the gray world of adulthood
everywhere, as though there never
had been any other, in that same house
I could not bear to leave, where even now
the child who wept to leave still sits
weeping at the thought of exile.

# WITNESS

An ordinary evening in Wisconsin
seen from a Greyhound bus—mute aisles
of merchandise the sole inhabitants
of the half-darkened Five and Ten,

the tables of the single lit café awash
with unarticulated pathos, the surface membrane
of the inadvertently transparent instant
when no one is looking : outside town

the barns, their red gone dark with sundown,
withhold the shudder of a warped terrain—
the castle rocks above, tree-clogged ravines
already submarine with nightfall, flocks

(like dark sheep) of toehold junipers,
the lucent arms of birches : purity
without a mirror, other than a mind bound
elsewhere, to tell it how it looks.

# FROM A CLINIC WAITING ROOM

I write from the denser enclave of the stricken,
eight stories up, a prairie *gratte-ciel*.
Above the valley floor, the bell tower
of a displaced Italian hill town listens, likewise
attentive to the mysteries of one Body.
If the two salute, it must be as monks do,
without gesture, eyes lowered
by the force of gravity. Between them,
down among the car parks, tree shapes
stripped twig-bare appear to bruise
with tenderness, illusory as sea anemones.
There is no wind. For days
the geese that winter in the bottomland
have been the one thing always on the move,
in swags of streaming fronds, chiaroscuro
sea blooms, their wavering V-signs
following the turnings of one body.
Where are they going?
                                    Down in the blood bank
the centrifuge, its branched transparent siphons
stripping the sap of Yggdrasil
from the slit arm of the donor, skims
the spinning corpuscles, cream-white
from hectic red. Below the pouched pack
dangled like a gout of mistletoe, the tubing
drips, drips from valve to valve to enter,
in a gradual procession, the cloistered
precincts of another body.
                                    Sunset, its tinctured
layerings vivid as delirium, astonishing
as merely to be living, stains the cold
of half a hemisphere. The old
moon's dark corpus, its mysteries
likewise halfway illusory, tonight sleeps slumped
on the phosphorescent threshold of the new.

# A CURFEW

*December 13, 1981*

Fever, the clang in the beleaguered pumproom
muffled with Tylenol, banked under icepacks,
rising while outside snow fell, a seeming flux
of strict constructions, the vapors' mimic
of turmoil among the leucocytes—mass panic,
blocked corridors, the riddlings of dispersal:
Why? If meaning is a part of any system,

what laws apply? To Alfred Wallace, burning
on his bed in the Moluccas, the malarial shimmer,
parting, whispered "Malthus": accident, disease,
war, famine certified as a severe epiphany, a random
elegance unfeeling as the Snow Queen's hex, the filter
of the future of the species. The stoic laughter
of Democritus: Nothing truly is except the atom,

the Whole a sieve of particles, its terrors
loomed of shadows' cumber. Along the thoroughfares
of Warsaw martial law, the day my brother died,
serried the pallid Baltic sun with roadblocks;
a curfew overtook the solstice. This winter, would
the sun turn round again for the gregarious gamble
of Solidarność? My brother dead, I cried over the news.

He'd looked into the murk of so much turmoil,
flux and rigor, unbought *pietàs* of the suicidal,
such jigsaw-fault-line fracturings of seeming
entity, fears of the action of God knew what laws
laid down by God knows who among the shadows
of the cave, the cloakroom or the bedroom—listening,
head down, eyes impassive, musing, feeling his way

along the pillared halls of withheld judgment—
and still, like a despairing small-hour phone call,
they trailed him down the fever's passageways
into the pumproom of delirium. "I think I won't
go to the office for a while," he murmured. "From
now on, just a few private patients." The snow fell,
the fever guttered, and the streets of Warsaw froze.

The thinnest of osmotic boundaries contain what once
was called the soul; the universal laws, the flux
of Heraclitus, packed yin-and-yangwise into the globule
of the infinitesimal, are now coöpted for a game of jacks,
taws toyed with by the hubris of a species whose petulant
*chevaux-de-frise* infest the globe with roadblocks,
a raging mimic of the universe's grand indifference.

# URN-BURIAL AND
# THE BUTTERFLY MIGRATION

Rest for the body's residue:
boxed ashes, earth pocket
under its lifted flap of turf
roofed by a black circumference
of Norway spruce, an old settler
now among old settlers, in their
numb stones' cooled silicates
the scar of memory benighted
alone articulate.

O friable repose of the organic!
Bark-creviced at the trunk's
foot, ladybirds' enameled herds
gather for the winter, red pearls
of an unsaid rosary to waking.
From the fenced beanfield,
crickets' brisk scrannel
plucks the worn reed of
individual survival.

Mulleins hunker to a hirsute
rosette about the taproot; from
frayed thistleheads, a liftoff
of aerial barbs begins; milkweed
spills on the wind its prodigal,
packed silks—slattern gondolas
whose wrecked stalks once
gave mooring to the sleep of
things terrestrial:

an urn of breathing jade, its
gilt-embossed exterior the
intact foreboding of a future
intricately contained, jet-
veined, spangle-margined,
birth-wet russet of the air-
traveling monarch emerging
from a torpid chrysalis. Oh,
we know nothing

of the universe we move through!
My dead brother, when we were
kids, fed milkweed caterpillars
in Mason jars, kept bees, ogled
the cosmos through a backyard
telescope. But then the rigor
of becoming throttled our pure
ignorance to mere haste
toward something else.

We scattered. Like the dandelion,
that quintessential successful
immigrant, its offspring gone
to fluff, dug-in hard-scrabble
nurtured a generation of
the mobile, nomads enamored
of cloverleafs, of hangars, of
that unrest whose home—*our*
home—is motion.

Here in the winds' terrain, the
glacier-abraded whetstone of their
keening knives, anvil of thunder,
its sabbaths one treacherous
long sob of apprehension, who
will rein in, harpoon or anchor
rest for the mind? Were the dead
to speak, were one day
these friable

residues to rise, would we hear
even that airborne murmur? Listen
as the monarchs' late-emerging
tribes ascend; you will hear
nothing. In wafted twos and threes
you may see them through the window
of a southbound Greyhound
bus, adrift across the
Minnesota border;

or in flickering clots, in dozens
above the parked cars of the
shopping malls of Kansas—this
miracle that will not live to
taste the scarce nectar, the
ample horror of another summer:
airborne marathon, elegiac
signature of nations who
have no language,

their landless caravans augment
among the blistered citadels
of Oklahoma; windborne along
the Dallas-Fort Worth airport's
utopian thoroughfares, their
hovering millenniums become
a mimic force of occupation,
a shadeless Vallombrosa,
forceless, autonomous.

O drifting apotheosis of dust
exhumed, who will unseal
the crypt locked up within
the shimmer of the chromosomes,
or harvest, from the alluvial
death-dance of these wrecked
galaxies, this risen residue
of milkweed leaf and honey,
rest for the body?

# THE COOLING TOWER

By night a laddered diagram
seen from the windows of this
bedroom town—rayflowers of dread
ascending and descending—
identifies the cooling tower,
insomniac vision

revealed by day as a grayed
obese archangel, its twiddled
dirk of ash and rhinestone
a metronomic rerun of some
half-obliterated last
nightmare of Eden

in the West: O Abendland, O
astral monochrome, steam-plume
whose throttled howl deploys
above the cooling tower
a pillared, effortless
volume of milkweed.

The air is windless. Harmless
outside the moat and continent of
power, the tabernacled rods'
implosive marrow, an aureole
of bright particulars let fall
falls unregarded,

such an excess as to be all but
sorrowless: the sumac's roadside
flares, used-car lots bannered as
for a gala, street maples' tattered
circus-tent extravaganza
sifting unnumbered

relics, emblems of the everywhere
expendable: O Abendland, astral
insomniac, prophetic hulk of the
unuttered: by whom, should your
hot hour arrive, will all the dreams
of Adam be remembered?

# A NEW LIFE

Autonomy these days—surprise!—is moving up
in the corporate structure. She's thrown over
the old laid-back lifestyle, repudiated its
green-haired prophets, and gotten married

(pre-Raphaelite red velvet, a sheaf of roses,
hair falling in two long blond tresses). She's
now at home on a rural route, its row of mailboxes
a mile and a half from the Freeway. Not-quite-

two-year-old Autonomy Junior spends long days
with the sitter, can count up to five, and sees
the world moving past so fast, he delivers daily
not slow words but quick, predicated word-clusters.

Up before dawn three days out of five, at the
bathroom mirror Autonomy swiftly, with brush and
hairdryer, concocts a frame for her face of that
temporal gold, like the gilding of the aspens

in the Rockies, like every prototypical true
blonde who began as some other color; puts on
her boardroom clothes—flounced denim with
boots and weskit, or spiked sandals and pallid

executive knit—to drive off into the just-
stirred mother-of-pearl of the day, the velour
of hoarfrost's transient platinum on the blacktop
of a piece with the pristine pale upholstery

of the brand-new Brougham—into the ductile
realm of the Freeway, that reentry into the mystery
of being betweenwheres, alone in the effortless
anteroom of the Machine, of the Many. The Company

these days is paying her way to an earlybird
course in Econ at the University. At eight-
thirty, while her wedded bedfellow, in the other
car, the red Toyota, drops off their offspring

with the sitter, her class over, she'll be taking
the Freeway again to headquarters. These days
she's in Quality Circles, a kind of hovering
equipoise between Management and not-Management,

precarious as the lake-twinned tremor of aspens,
as the lingering of the ash-blond arcade of foliage
completing itself as it leans to join its own inversion.
Whatever fabrication, whatever made thing

she is thus vertiginously linked to, there's no
disconnecting the image of Autonomy contained but
still moving—toward what is unclear—up through
the heady apertures of the Gross National Product,

from that thing, the ambiguous offspring of the Company—
through whose dense mansions, burbling with unheard
melodies of the new, her pal and bedfellow is moving up too.
Evenings, while he heads for *his* course at the University,

she collects the not-yet-two-year-old from the sitter,
kicks off her stiltwalker's footgear, peels away
the layers of the persona she takes to Quality Circles,
and slides into irontight jeans, the time-honored

armor of mellowing out; picks up yesterday's litter
around the playpen, puts together a quick concoction
via the microwave oven, and resumes—her charge,
all the while, voluble at her hip or underfoot—

the improbable game of move-and-countermove-between-
mother-and-child. Whether, back at headquarters,
back there in the winking imaginary map that leaps
from the minds of the computer programmers, there's

a mother-lode of still smarter bombs, the germ
of an even cleverer provocation to instability
within the neutron or of God knows what other, yet
inviolate speck at the core of the cosmos, who knows—

or whether playing at mothering, the mirage of a
rise into ethereal realms of the managerial—of
hoarfrost at dawn along the edge of the Freeway,
the hurtled ease of finding oneself betweenwheres,

alone in the evolving anteroom of the Machine, of
that artifice of the pursuit of happiness—will be,
as the green-haired prophets of punk would have it,
a total, or only a partial
                              apocalyptic freakout.

The geranium and the begonia
bloom with such offhand redundance
we scarcely notice. But the
amaryllis is a study in

disruption: everything routine
gives way to the unsheathing
of its climbing telescope—
a supernova of twin crimson

tunnels, porches of infinity
where last week there was nothing.
Months of clandestine preparation
now implode in pollen

that will never brush a bee,
fueling the double-barreled velvet
stairwell of its sterile pistils
with a tapered incandescence

that's already short of breath
and going blind before a
week is out. Such show
of breeding, such an excess

of cultivation, all but asks us
to stop breathing too until
it's over. I remember
how, the night the somewhat

famous violinist came to supper,
the whisper of the gown she
put on just before the concert
filled the parlor of the farmhouse

with things it had no room for—
the slave marts of the East,
the modes of Paris, the gazing
ramparts of the stratosphere.

# III

## VOYAGES:
## A HOMAGE TO JOHN KEATS

*for Helen Vendler*

Cowslip and shad-blow, flaked like tethered foam
Around bared teeth of stallions, bloomed that spring
When I first read the lines, rife as the loam
Of prairies, yet like breakers cliffward leaping!
  . . . My hand
                    in yours,
                            Walt Whitman . . .
                            —Hart Crane, *The Bridge*


Chaff, straw, splinters of wood, weeds, and the sea-gluten,
Scum, scales from shining rocks, leaves of salt-lettuce, left by the tide,
Miles walking, the sound of breaking waves the other side of me,
Paumanok there and then I thought the old thought of likenesses,
These you presented to me you fish-shaped island . . .
                            —Walt Whitman, *Sea Drift*


Perhaps my whisper was already born before my lips,
the leaves whirled round in treelessness
and those to whom we dedicate our life's experience
before experience acquired their traits.
                            —Osip Mandelstam
                              (Moscow, January 1934)


. . . a haggling of wind and weather, by these lights
Like a blaze of summer straw, in winter's nick.
                            —Wallace Stevens,
                              *The Auroras of Autumn*

Reading his own lines over, he'd been
(he wrote) in the diminished state of one
"that gathers Samphire dreadful trade."
Disabled Gloucester, so newly eyeless
all his scathed perceptions bled together,
and Odysseus, dredged up shipwrecked
through fathoms of Homeric sightlessness—

"the sea had soaked his heart through"—
were the guides his terror clutched at.
Now all of twenty-one, he'd written nothing
of moment but one bookish sonnet: "Much have
I traveled . . ." Only he hadn't, other
than as unrequited amateur. How clannish
the whole hand-to-hand, cliffhanging trade,

the gradual letdown, the hempen slither,
precarious basketloads of sea drift
gathered at Margate or at Barnegat:
along Paumanok's liquid rim, the dirges,
nostalgia for the foam: *the bottom of
the sea is cruel.* The chaff, the scum
of the impalpable confined in stanzas,

a shut-in's hunger for the bodiless
enkindlings of the aurora—all that
traffic in the perilous. That summer,
orphaned of sublimity, he'd settled for
the way an oatfield's stalks and blades
checquered his writing tablet with their
quivering. But after, back in Hampstead,

the samphire-gatherer's mimic god-deliverer
still bled metonymy: an ordinary field of
barley turned to alien corn's inland sea-
surfaces, and onto every prairie rolling,
sans the samphire trade's frail craft, un-
basketed, undid the casement of the homesick,
stared once more, and called an image home.

Even in mild Devon, that spring, the lung-
destroying English climate was one long
dank rampage: high winds, trees falling
onto the roads, stagecoaches overturning,

day upon day of drumming, streaming rain
swollen to weeks, the sun a half-believed-in
pagan god above the azure of the Mediterranean.
At night he'd lie in bed (he wrote) and listen

to it with a sense of being drowned and rotted
like a grain of wheat. He very nearly hated
Tom because he coughed so; then his raw mood
froze as he saw his brother cough up blood.

His writing plodded. By now *Endymion* bored him.
His letters joked of waterspouts and rattraps. Rhyme,
that light-fingered habit, ran down and went grim:
beyond an untumultuous fringe of foam,

he'd seen, once the weather eased, into a maw
of rot, a predatory core of dying. Melodrama
mildewed the sources of romance: the basil grew
rank from her dead lover's skull for Isabella.

What might still flower out of that initiation
to the sodden underside of things—those Eleusinian
passageways that seem (he wrote) only to darken
as the doors of new and vaster chambers open—

he could no more than guess at. On May Day
he looked from the window of a single stanza
leaning toward Theocritus and the blue Bay
of Baiae (read Naples). Not yet twenty-three,

he'd presently begin to resurrect, to all but
deify the issue of his own wretched climate—
primroses, cress and water-mint, great wet-
globed peonies, the grape against the palate:

an *annus mirabilis* of odes before the season
of the oozing of the ciderpress, the harvest done,
wheatfields blood-spattered once with poppies gone
to stubble now, the swallows fretting to begin

their windborne flight toward a Mediterranean
that turned to marble as the mists closed in
on the imagination's yet untrodden region—
the coal-damps, the foul winter dark of London.

# THE ELGIN MARBLES

*For Frederick Turner*

Openings. Winandermere and Derwentwater.
The Elgin Marbles. That last evening
at the Crown in Liverpool, with George
and his new wife, imagination failed

    —and still fails: what can John Keats
    have had to do with a hacked clearing
    in the Kentucky underbrush? How could
    Mnemosyne herself, the mother of the Muse,
    have coped with that uncultivated tangle,
    catbrier and poison ivy, chiggers,
    tent caterpillars, cottonmouths,
    the awful gurglings and chirrings
    of the dark?

                  Turning his back
against the hemp and tar, the
creaking tedium of actual departure,
the angry fogs, the lidless
ferocity of the Atlantic—epic
distances fouled by necessity—
he left them sleeping, George
and his Georgiana, so much wrapped up
in being newly wed they scarcely knew
they had no home now but each other,
he took up his pack (a change of
clothes, pens, paper, the *Divine
Comedy* in translation—he knew no
Italian yet, or Greek) and headed north,
on foot, with his friend Brown. Rain
held them up a day, but on
the twenty-sixth of June (a letter

to his brother Tom records) they came
in sight of Winandermere. He stared,
then slowly swore, "This—
must—beat—Italy."

                    Imaginary
Italy, the never-never
vista, framed, of Stresa
on Lago Maggiore, to badger
an imagination starved for charm,
for openings, living on cornpone,
coonskin, literary hand-me-downs,
and hating everything in sight.

                    Hyperbole:
a vista, as he put it, to make one forget
what tended to cut off, refining what he called
the Sensual Vision into—he fumbled for
an image—a sort of North Star, open-
lidded, steadfast. Winandermere:
the Italy he'd never seen, though in
imagination he already lived there:
his mind's America. Bright star.
Made one forget the creak, the tar,
the lunging hulk, homesick, sea-
sick, of the Atlantic.

                    Or almost did.
Next day, at Helvellyn (mist about its foot
so thick he never saw it, the Nag's Head
flea-infested) he invoked,
in an acrostic on Georgiana's name, Odysseus
stormed at sea, and after

Derwentwater and Lodore made weak amends
with fact by conjuring a doggerel prospect
"where furrows are new to the plow."
After Skiddaw—a ten-mile hike,
made fasting, having gotten up
at four—they took a coach
for Scotland.

                  The tomb of Burns.
Pinched lives. Bad food. A fog
of whisky. The cold, pale, short-
lived, primeval summer. He was tired now,
homesick for another kind of grandeur:
Lord Elgin's windlass-lowered metopes ("A sun—
a shadow of a magnitude," he'd written
of the space they opened). Scotland
seemed—the epithet broke from him—
*anti-Grecian*. Admitting prejudice,
he repented, tried whisky-toddy,
wrote a ballad, saw the poverty, grew somber
as he thought of Burns, observing his imagination
had been southern too; caught a cold
he couldn't shake, grew peevish,
cut short his tour. In Hampstead,
Tom had been coughing blood again.

                           Another
summer gone, Tom worse, his own sore throat
recurring, *Endymion* stillborn, picked over
by the vultures. Well,
they were partly right; the rest he wouldn't
think about. Now, primed on *Lear*,
Milton, Gibbon, Wordsworth, he'd set himself

to re-imagining an epic grandeur, such as
(if it arrived at all) came battered
and diminished, fallen like Lucifer,
or else dismantled, fragmentary, lowered and
transported, piece by piece, like the heroic
torsos, the draperied recumbent hulks Lord Elgin
took down from the Parthenon.

        —Behold,
 in the back settlements, the rise
 of Doric porticoes. Courthouse
 spittoons. The glimmer of a classic
 colonnade through live oaks. Slave
 cabins. Mud. New Athenses, Corinths,
 Spartas among the Ossabaws and
 Tuscaloosas, the one no less
 homesick than the other for
 what never was, most likely,
 but in some founder's warped
 and sweating mind.

       Ruin alone,
in a bad time, had seemed to him
grand enough. But then, out of the
still unimagined West, that welter
of a monument to hardship, stirrings
of another sort: Georgiana
was to have a child.

        Precarious
domestic comfort, a firelit
ring of faces' bright cave
in the Kentucky wilderness: the wonder

of it! Not quite two years
since, in lodgings he and George and Tom,
three orphaned, homeless brothers
had moved into, he'd invoked
just such an image: small, busy flames
playing through fresh-laid
coals, a refuge hollowed from
the gloom of London in November. Now,
out of that solitude, a child,
another Keats, to be the bard of what
John Keats himself could never quite
imagine: he turned the fantasy
into a lullaby, went back
to reconstructing such an inlet
to severe magnificence
as a god might enter. "I think
I shall be among the English
poets after my death." There,
he'd said it.

        The evening of
October twenty-fourth (a date that,
once again, would go on record),
walking from Bedford Row to Lamb's
Conduit Street, he met the enigmatic
Mrs. Isabella Jones, and walked her home.
Her sitting room a trove of bronze,
books, pictures, music (an Aeolian
harp, a linnet): rich and somber—moonlight
through diamond panes, a Turkish carpet—
was the way he'd re-imagine it. A
prior contretemps seemed to require
some move. Tactfully declining to

be kissed, however, she released him
to a state of mind that was—
he discovered, walking home
astonished—infinitely
better:
                    *He was free.*
He could imagine anything at all,
needed no home, would never marry—not
though the carpet there were silk,
the curtain made of morning cloud, with windows
that opened on Winandermere. The roaring
of the wind, he wrote (hyperbole again, but
never mind) would be his wife, the stars
seen through the windows would be his children.
A perfect solitude. A thousand worlds thrown open
He was as happy as a man could be—or would be,
he conscientiously amended, if Tom were better.

Bright star. Winandermere. A week
from now, he would be twenty-three.

There would have been the obligatory tour
of the cathedral. Stone under boot heels,
the great, numbed ribcage chilled-to-the-bone
cold. The aisles of sculptured effigies stone
dead. Tom dead at the beginning of December.
It was January now. Buried at St. Stephen's
Coleman Street. The bare spire, the leafless
trees. The church bells' interminable reminder.
One Sunday evening, hearing them, he'd dashed
off—with Tom there in the room, timing him—
a sonnet "In Disgust of Vulgar Superstition."
Here, the recurrent chatter of those great
metal tongues would have brought it back,
setting his memory on edge again. *Poor Tom*.
The scene out on the heath forever lurking
in his mind. Back in October he'd underlined
the words: Poor Tom. Poor Tom's a-cold.

His friends meant well, had kept him occupied.
Visits. A play. Dragged him down to Sussex
for a prizefight. Mrs. Isabella Jones, with
new notions for him to write about. Miss
Brawne: beautiful, elegant, graceful, silly,
fashionable and strange. He'd set down the
words with care. It was important to keep
things accurate. A minx—he'd called her
that, and also ignorant, monstrous in her
behavior, flying out in all directions, calling
people such names. Hair nicely arranged.
Loved clothes. Eighteen years old. Down here,
best not to think very much about her. Brown
playing the fool, putting on an old lady's
bonnet. At night, old dowager card parties.
As always, the anxiety about getting down

to work. No progress with the epic since Tom
died. Isabella Jones urging him to try another
romance. Why not, she'd said, the legend
of St. Agnes' Eve? A girl going to bed . . .

He must have whistled at the notion that struck
him now. And then blushed. Or vice versa. A
girl going to bed on St. Agnes' Eve—that very
night, or near it—without supper, so as to
dream of the man she was to marry. Imagine
her. Imagine . . . He blushed now at the
audacity. But the thing had taken hold:
St. Agnes' Eve. A girl going to bed . . .
On the twenty-third of January, they walked
thirteen miles, to a little town called (of
all things) Bedhampton. The house they stayed
in there still stands. Out of the frozen
countryside they'd passed through, once his
numb hands had thawed, he had what he needed
to begin: the owl, the limping hare, the
woolly huddle inside the sheepfold. Even
the owl a-cold. *Poor Tom.* The cold stone
underfoot, the sculptured effigies. How
they must ache. His own numb fingers. How
the Beadsman's hands must ache. Paid to hold
a rosary for the souls of others richer and
more vicious. The stones he knelt on cold.
The girl's bedchamber cold, the bed itself
too, until the girl—blushing, he saw her
kneel—had warmed it. He saw it all.

He saw it: saw the candle in the icy draft
gone out, the little smoke, the moonlight,
the diamond panes, the stained-glass colors
on her as she knelt to say her silly prayers.

Saw her, smelled her, felt the warmth of the
unfastened necklace, the brooch, the earrings,
heard the rustle as the dress slid down;
backed off, became the voyeur of a mermaid.
Discovered, while she slept, that the sheets
gave off a sachet of lavender. Admired but
did not taste the banquet his senses had
invented, and whose true name was Samarkand.
He was in fact too excited to eat. What is
a poet to do when he stumbles onto such
excitement? He was not sure. He was also
somewhat embarrassed. Later he'd declare,
hotly, that he wrote for men, not ladies
(who are the ones who dream such things),
that he'd despise any man who was such a
eunuch as not to avail himself . . . It was
the flaw, as he must have known. He'd
imagined it all. He'd imagined it all.

For ten days that lush, decorated stanza,
with its shut casements and dying fall,
had been the room he lived in. He'd
imagined it all; his senses had seduced
an entire posterity into imagining what
had never happened. His own virgin vision,
of a solitude that needed no wife, had been
seduced by that imaginary place, that stanza,
where nothing at all had happened. The minx
who was eighteen, beautiful, silly, strange
and fond of clothes, and who had never lived
there, was real. The cold outside was real.
Dying was real, and the twitch of the old
woman's palsy. The effigies were real,
and the stones in the churchyard at St.
Stephen's Coleman Street. *Poor Tom.*

The April he'd invoked from the despond
of February (when his sore throat
came back)—its hillsides starred
by an upended firmament of daisies—
found him straining at particles of
light in a great darkness, bright-eyed
underfoot with scurryings of purpose:
the alert stoat, the quivering fieldmouse,
the lowlife fracases he'd seen erupting
in the streets of London—instinct in
the bud, the blood stirred in a poor
forked creature battered by the same
mischances, subject to the same
　　　　inclement weather.

On the eleventh day of April he
shook the hand of Coleridge, and
felt warmed. But the low mood that
had hampered him continued. *Hyperion,*
he knew now after a final try—*Apollo
shrieked—and lo! from all his limbs
celestial* . . . would not be completed.
How could he not think with irony of
that *celestial*? The foreign sun-god,
aloof familiar of the Muse, once-blazing
luminary now a mere pinprick, remote
among the other stars—himself left
shivering, abandoned to the merciless
catarrhs of London. Infernal visions
drew him: not now that scathing splendor,
the lyre, the paean, the white glare
of sunstruck marble, but the wailing
shades, the cranes' cry, the starlings
interminably circling: imagined torments
　　　　of felicity remembered.

April in hell, a courteous reception
to the circle of the lustful: the dream
he'd had came back as pure enjoyment.
Welcomed by Francesca, late of Rimini,
into the storm of starlings, joined
to another solely by a kiss, for what
had seemed an aeon's celestial levitation,
he had been happy: in the midst of all
that cold and darkness, *he was warm.*
April in hell: a firmament upended
to a stirred greensward of treetops
that, tiptoe, he felt expanding into
secret zodiacs of blossom. And then
       woke. And shivered.

Outside, it was raining. He stayed in
all day, attempting in a sonnet—"Pale
were the lips I kissed"—to summon
back the dream. Damp, half-charred
firewood brought in from the rain,
it wouldn't kindle—until, on the
twenty-first of April, in an aubade
set to the starved meter of a ballad,
he harpooned the levitating kiss, and
quartered it. (Why *four* kisses?—Because,
he quipped, the Muse needs reining in.
Suppose I had said seven?) So adieu,
Francesca, late of Rimini. Farewell,
imaginary region of the headlong; even
your lusts cannot (it seems) delude so well
as the received morality would have it.
Dream of being warm, farewell.
Exposure on a cold hillside,
       good morning.

April long gone, the sedges dead
and withered: wake, poor fool, to agues
of the morning after—to having been,
from your brief *saison en enfer*,
locked out, the ecstasy aborted,
masked Melancholy's sable domino
torn off, the Muse herself disclosed,
in the strict morning light, as an
unforthcoming warden: no comfort,
only carnage underfoot, a cutthroat
cunning prowling the streets of
London—and waking, one among
the many, from dim dreams, harbored
numberless as vermin, of being warm,
to freezing on this houseless,
      flowerless hillside.

# THE ISLE OF WIGHT

Toward the end of April, for an idyllic
　　week, the rain stopped, and on the third
of May he wrote, "O there is nothing like
　　fine weather, health, Books, a contented
Mind . . ." The ballad's nightmare hillside
　　turned, on a burst of bloom, into a picnic:
Psyche, poor butterfly-winged, put-upon immortal,
　　last met with in the cold of that starved bedrock,
translated, bless her, to shameless daylit *al*
　　*fresco*, the flowery upheaval of the marriage bed.

Reclaimed thus for Eros, what had he to offer?
　　Rash promises, no more. He'd build (he wrote)
a sanctuary purely of the mind, in some far-
　　off, untrodden region, with a window in it
left open every night, not now to frame
　　the stars (if any) but to admit a visitor
prohibited the homelier usages of daylight.
　　A sanctuary of the mind, no more. That summer,
cooped with a Bacchic leopard on the Isle of Wight,
　　he'd wish he'd never offered it house room.

"Ask yourself my love whether you are not
　　very cruel to have so destroyed my freedom,"
he wrote—hyperbole such as he'd often laughed at.
　　But now he'd let this hot sprite in, the gloom
of sundown brought home, night after night,
　　to that room he said was like a coffin,
no ornate access such as had beguiled him—
　　no casement triple-arched as on the night,
long gone, those lovers fled into the storm:
　　the framework of escape had shut him in.

His sore throat had come back in June; he saw
    still no prospect of a settled income,
could not live with her but could not now sue
    love for a retraction. Shut up with phantom
rivals in that little room at Shanklin,
    where was the old, wild pleasure of a window
opening on a view of water?—Sealed off like a poem
    he might have written once but couldn't now—
its magic casements closed against the spume
    and spindrift of a serpentine illusion.

Illusion, snared in a brisk running couplet,
    was his new preoccupation—the dazed lamé
of its phosphorescent moons, its shivering scarlet
    and skewered emeralds a weird trophy
hung among the totems of his own ambivalence:
    he almost yearned, he'd written at the start,
for metempsychosis as an insect—for just three
    butterfly-winged summer days' intensity. *Delight*,
he'd called it: poor worn-out word. Poor Psyche,
    poor feeble suffix of doubtful provenance!

# WINCHESTER:
# THE AUTUMN EQUINOX

Salubrious air, free of the low fogs that were
(he wrote) like steam from cabbage water;
past scrubbed stoops and ram's-head-knockered
doors, a daily walk through the cathedral yard
down to the river: how beautiful
the season was—ay, better than
the chilly green of spring, the warmed hue
of grainfields' harsh stubs turned pictorial
with equinoctial bloom, the tincture of
the actual, the mellow aftermath of fever:
purgatorial winnowings, the harvest over.

Seamless equipoise of crossing: Nox,
primordial half-shape above the treadle,
the loomed fabric of the sun-god's ardor
foreshortened, with a roar as if of earthly
fire, all twilit Europe at his back,
toward the threshold of the west: *in me*
*thou seest such twilight, in me thou seest*
*the glowing of such fire as after sunset*
floods the west's unentered spaces. Black gates
shut against the sunrise; north and south, a mist
of nothing: the opening was to the west.

The opening of the West: what Miltonic
rocketry of epithet, what paradigm
of splendor in decline, could travel,
and survive, the monstrous region (as he'd
later depict it) of dull rivers poured
from sordid urns, rank tracts unowned
by any weed-haired god he'd ever heard of,
that had fleeced his brother George? "Be careful,"

he wrote, "of those Americans"—meaning
mainly a certain Audubon, of Henderson,
Kentucky. "I can not help thinking Mr. Audubon

has deceived you. I shall not like the sight
of him. . . . You will perceive," he'd also
written, "it is quite out of my interest to
come to America. What could I do there? How
could I employ myself?" John James Audubon,
whether swindler or merely incorrigibly careless,
might carve a kind of wonder, a fierce, frightful
elegance, out of the houseless openings,
the catbrier-hammock deadfalls of that
unfenced paradise. But what could Milton,
from whom he'd set himself to learn, have done

to clear a path either for grandeur or
for simple ruth to enter? Look homeward—
where? What images, what language, fossil
child of all the dislocations of antiquity,
could clear that threshold? *Like the mild moon
who comforts those she sees not, who knows not
what eyes are upward cast*, Moneta, Shade
of Memory, Admonisher, when called upon—
whereon (he wrote) *there grew a power within me
of enormous ken*—showed only splendor fallen.
His peace made with the diminishments of autumn,

he now declared the second epic of the sun-
god's fall abandoned.
                              Hampstead: Fever
and passion. A comedy. A sonnet. In letters,
now and then a cry of protest. The rest
is posthumous.

On April twenty-seventh, 1932, Hart Crane
walked to the taffrail of the *Orizaba*,
took off his coat, and leaped. At seventeen,
a changeling from among the tire-and-rubber

factories, steel mills, cornfields of the Ohio
flatland that had absent-mindedly produced him,
on an enthralled first voyage he'd looked into
the troughed Caribbean, and called it home.

Back where he'd never been at home, he'd once
watched the early-morning shift pour down South Main—
immigrant Greeks eager to be Americans—
and then tried to imagine Porphyro in Akron

(Greek for "high place"): the casement, the arras,
the fabricated love nest, the actual sleet storm,
the owl, the limping hare, the frozen grass,
Keats's own recurring dream of being warm—

who'd been so often cold he looked with yearning even
into blacksmiths' fires: "How glorious," he wrote
of them, shivering (with Stevens) to see the stars put on
their glittering belts: of what disaster was that

chill, was that salt wind the imminence? The cold-
a-long-time, lifetime snow man did not know.
Beside the Neva, Osip Mandelstam wrote of the cold,
the December fog-blurs of Leningrad. O to throw

open (he wrote) a window on the Adriatic!—a window
for the deprived of audience, for the unfree
to breathe, to breathe even the bad air of Moscow.
Yet on the freezing pane of perpetuity,

that coruscating cold-frame fernery of breath,
harsh flowerbed of the unheated rooms of childhood,
even from the obscurity that sealed it off, his breath,
his warmth, he dared declare, had already settled.

The dream of being warm, its tattered cargo
brought too late to Italy, a mere dire fistful
of blood (*the sea had soaked his heart through*):
the voyage, every voyage at the end is cruel.

In February 1937, from exile to flatland
Voronezh, a kind of twin of Akron, Mandelstam
wrote, in an almost posthumous whisper, of round
blue bays, of sails descried—scenes parted from

as now his voyage to the bottom of a crueler
obscurity began, whose end only the false-haired
seaweed of an inland shipwreck would register.
Untaken voyages, Lethean cold, O all but unendured

arrivals! Keats's starved stare before the actual,
so long imagined Bay of Naples. The mind's extinction.
Nightlong, sleepless beside the Spanish Steps, the prattle
of poured water. Letters no one will ever open.

# IV

## THE METROPOLIS

# THE REEDBEDS
# OF THE HACKENSACK

Scummed maunderings that nothing loves but reeds,
*Phragmites*, neighbors of the greeny asphodel
that thrive among the windings of the Hackensack,
collaborating to subvert the altogether ugly
though too down-to-earth to be quite fraudulent:
what's landfill but the backside of civility?

Dreckpot, the Styx and Malebolge of civility,
brushed by the fingering plumes of beds of reeds:
Manhattan's moat of stinks, the rancid asphodel
aspiring from the gradually choking Hackensack,
ring-ditch inferior to the vulgar, the snugly ugly,
knows-no-better, fake but not quite fraudulent:

what's scandal but the candor of the fraudulent?
Miming the burnish of a manicured civility,
the fluent purplings of uncultivated reeds,
*ex post cliché* survivors like the asphodel,
drink, as they did the Mincius, the Hackensack
in absent-minded benediction on the merely ugly.

Is there a poetry of the incorrigibly ugly,
free of all furbishings that mark it fraudulent?
When toxins of an up-against-the-wall civility
have leached away the last patina of these reeds,
and promised landfill, with its lethal asphodel
of fumes, blooms the slow dying of the Hackensack,

shall I compare thee, Mincius, to the Hackensack?
Now Italy knows how to make its rivers ugly,
must, ergo, all such linkages be fraudulent,

gilding the laureate hearse of a defunct civility?
Smooth-sliding Mincius, crowned with vocal reeds,
coevals of that greeny local weed the asphodel,

that actual, unlettered entity the asphodel,
may I, among the channels of the Hackensack—
those Edens-in-the-works of the irrevocably ugly,
where any mourning would of course be fraudulent—
invoke the scrannel ruth of a forsooth civility,
the rathe, the deathbed generations of these reeds?

# BURIAL IN CYPRESS HILLS

*For Beverly and Lloyd Barzey*

Back through East Flatbush, a raw grave
littered by the trashing of the social contract,
to this motel of the dead, its plywood and acrylic
itching gimcrack Hebrew like a brand name.

Her case botched by a vandal of a Brooklyn doctor,
she'd readied everything, had all the old snapshots
sorted, down to the last mysterious interior
obliterated in the processes of coming clear.

Surprising, the amount of privacy that opens,
for all the lifetime rub of other people,
around a name uncertified by being in the papers—
one mainly of the bilked, who never formed a party—

and how unhandsome the nub of actual survival.
Nobody is ever ready for the feel of the raw edge
between being and nothing, the knowledge
that abrades the palm, refusing to lie easy.

Yet something in the way the sun shines even now,
out in the open, on that final nugget, makes
bereavement blithe. The undertaker's deputy,
getting the latest lot of mourners into cars,

barks like a sergeant, as though even limbo must
be some new sort of boot camp. "Brooklyn people"—
one of the cousins sums it all up, without rancor:
a way of doing business, part of the local color.

Burial in Cypress Hills, a place whose avenues
are narrower than anywhere in Brooklyn: dark-
boled gateposts crowded elbow to elbow,
the woodlot of innumerable burial societies,

each pair of verticals dense as a tenement
with names, or as a column in the *Daily Forward*.
Whoever enters here to take up residence
arrives an immigrant, out of another country.

The cortege, one of many, inches forward, no more
to be hurried than at Ellis Island. On foot now,
we find the yellow cellar hole, a window into clay,
without a sill, whose only view is downward.

Time, for the gravediggers, is unarguably money:
the cadence of their lifted shovelfuls
across the falling phrases of the Kaddish
strikes on a rarely opened vein of metal

whose pure ore rings like joy, although that's not
the name we've been conditioned into giving it.
Around us, flowering trees hang their free fabric,
incorporeal as the act of absolution. At our feet

an unintended dandelion breaks the hasp
of the adjoining plot's neglected ivy
to spend ungrudgingly its single
fringed medallion, alms for the sun.

# THE GODFATHER
## RETURNS TO COLOR TV

The lit night glares like a day-glo strawberry,
the stakeout car beside the hydrant is full of feds,
and the ikon of our secret hero(ine?), atop the
feckless funnypaper mesa we try to live in, is that
poor dumb indestructible super-loser Krazy Kat.

O Innocence, spoiled Guinea Brat!—after whose
fits of smashing and screaming, O Holy Mother,
All-American Girl, I need you, I want
to protect you: after that one sunstruck
glimpse, on a Sicilian mountainside,

of virgin stupidity, its sensual lockbox
so charged with possibilities of being
that we too tremble at the thought of nakedness,
of marriage, we too burn to build a shrine for,
raise armies to protect a property that history

godfathered dumb. I told you: DON'T ASK
QUESTIONS ABOUT MY BUSINESS! While the old
bull in a new world, who's lost respect,
too-big pants bunched underneath the belly, stumbles
expiring past the staked tomato vines,

and the grandchild thinks for a minute he's
only playing, we *know* he is, admiring
Marlon Brando in a show of weakness. But the blood
isn't all ketchup, or the weekend all football, nor
do all commodities survive in lighted shrines.

O Italy! Imagine Eros reinvented on that hillside
as Giovanni di Paolo did—a passeggiata
where men and women walk into the day ungoaded,
unprotected, unenshrined—while we make do, stranded
on this day-glo mesa, with its epicene cartoon.

# REAL ESTATE

Something there is that doesn't
love a Third Avenue tenement,

that wants it gone the way the El
went. Façade a typical example

of red-brick eclectic, its five dozen
windows half now behind blank tin,

scrollwork lintels of strange parentage,
fire escapes' curling-iron birdcage,

are an anomaly among high-rise elevators,
besieged by Urban Relocation (Not A

Governmental Agency). Holdout tenants
confer, gesticulating, by storefronts

adapted only to an anxious present—Le
Boudoir, Le Shampoo, Le Retro (if passé

is chic, is chic passé?). One gelded
pawnshop, until last week, still brooded,

harboring, among tag ends of pathos,
several thirty-year-old umbrellas.

Regularly twice a day, the lingering wraith
within stepped out to shake her dustcloth.

That's done now. She advertised a sale.
Still nothing moved. Finally, a U-Haul

truck carted everything off somewhere.
Hail, real estate! Bravo, entrepreneur!

# A SCAFFOLD

*J'entends déjà tomber avec des chocs funèbres*
*Le bois retentissant sur le pavé des cours.*
      —Baudelaire, "Chant d'Automne"


The lumbering chords that open
    a Beethoven sonata,
the autumnal thump of cordwood
    Baudelaire, with a

premonitory shiver, heard unloaded
    in a Paris courtyard;
the offstage axe precipitately ringing down
    the cherry orchard

before the trunks are packed: what woke us,
    cleaving the usual
matutinal cacophony, inexorable as a
    wrecker's ball, was all

of these: the *choc funèbre* of a hard-
    hat hammerklavier,
the latest demolition crew whose live-
    lihood requires, before

they can ring down, irrevocably as
    a scuttled stage set,
the tenement whose last holdouts have been
    pried out like crabmeat—

I watched their banished chattels go,
    the sick pianoforte
with its jangled nerves, the purblind allegori-
    cal museum copy—

the raising of a scaffold (Baudelaire,
     his ear infallibly
tuned to foreboding, was already there
     to hear that echo),

a sidewalk arcade, a makeshift footing
     for the executioners,
a floor for a cowcatcher crèche, a flange
     made of dismantled doors,

a coffin (Baudelaire, needless to say, was
     also on hand to hear
it put together, blow added to blow,
     shudder to shudder)

for the last remains of rooms—
     the beams, the falling
lath and plaster—whose only crime was
     hanging on too long.

# VACANT LOT WITH
# TUMBLEWEED AND PIGEONS

The rooms gone, hallways and stairwells
air, the cornices and fire escapes
where troops of sunning pigeons spun
from common-garden opalescence
the transience of some other thing
more rich and strange, two summers
and a winter solstice since

a dozen dumpsterloads of rubble dis-
embodied what had once seemed settled
here, effaced: the ricepaper
of the first December snowfall
inscribed with a not-yet-uprooted
tumbleweed's whip-limber pyramid,
spare, see-through, symmetrical,

an evergreen in one dimension, each
brushed-in, accidental grass-stroke
beside it letter perfect. Two
summers and a winter solstice
since their perching places went,
pigeons still arrive from somewhere,
and as in a liturgy retrace,

descending yet again the roofless
staircase of outmoded custom, the
soon-to-be-obliterated stations
of nostalgia—as though the air
itself might wince at the stigmata
of the dispossessed, the razed,
the *triste*, the unaccounted-for.

# RINGING DOORBELLS

that night for Gene
McCarthy at the edge
of Little Italy
turned into
an olfactory
adventure: after

the mildew, after
the musts and fetors
of tomcat and cockroach,
barrooms' beer-reek,
the hayfield whiff
of pot, hot air

of laundromats
a flux of borax,
the entire effluvium
of the polluted
Hudson opened
like a hidden

fault line, and from
a cleft between the
backs of buildings
blossomed, out of
the dark, as
with hosannas,

the ageless,
pristine, down-
to-earth aromas
of tomorrow's
bread from
Zito's Bakery.

# TOWNHOUSE INTERIOR
## WITH CAT

*For Joan and Dean McClure*

Green-gold, the garden leans into the room,
the room leans out into the garden's
hanging intertwine of willow. Voluptuous
on canvas, arum lilies' folded cream
rises on its own green undertone. The walls
are primrose; needlepoint-upholstered
walnut and, underfoot, a Bokhara heirloom
bring in the woodwind resonance of autumn.
Mirrored among jungle blooms' curled crimson
and chartreuse, above the mantel, diva-throated
tuberoses, opening all the stops, deliver
Wagnerian arias of perfume.
                                    The kettle
warbles in the kitchen; we take our teacups
downstairs to where the willow harbors,
improbably, a ring of mushrooms. Tulips
and rhododendrons have almost done blooming;
laced overhead, neighboring locust trees
discard their humid ivory.
                                    But where's
the favorite with the green-gold headlamps?
She's perverse today; declines, called out
of hiding, to recall past tête-à-têtes
of sparring hand-to-paw; claws up a tree;
patrols a wall. We see her disappear
into her own devices. Cornered later
under the gateleg table, tail aloof,
she flirts, an eloquence of fur, but won't

be wooed or flattered. The look she gives
me, when she looks—the whole green-gold,
outdoor-indoor continuum condensed
to a reproachful pair of jewels—is wild
and scathingly severe.

# TIME

It may be we are in the last days.
Seven hundred years ago to the week,
on the eleventh of December, the kingdom of Wales went under.
Today, the sixth day of the twelfth month of the nineteen hundred
    eighty-second year, according to the current reckoning,
there are roses the size of an obsolete threepenny bit—
one fingernail-pink, the other minute, extravagant crimson—
flanked by masses of sweet alyssum
and one time-exempt purple pansy
on the site of what was formerly the Women's House of Detention
at the triangular intersection of Tenth Street with Greenwich and
    Sixth Avenues,
just back of the old Jefferson Market courthouse
whose tower clock, revived, goes on keeping time.
And I think again of October violets,
of their hardy refusal to adhere to conventional expectation—
so hardy that I've finally ceased to think of it as startling,
this phenomenon which, in fact, I devoted myself in October to
    looking for—
a tame revenant of the blue fire-alarm of the original encounter
    with the evidence,
among the dropped leaves and superannuated grass of the season
    of hickory nuts,
that neither time nor place could be counted on to remain
    self-sufficient,
that you might find yourself slipping back toward the past at any
    moment,
or watch it well up in artesian springs of anachronism,
with the prospect of being drowned in that aperture's abrupt blue,
in that twinkling of an eye, at any moment.
It was November, or near then, I found violets massed at the foot
    of the foundations of the castle of Chepstow,
at the edge of Wales—not any longer, as once, covert, fecklessly
    undermining

that sense of fitness, so fragile that at any moment of one's
    childhood
whatever sense of continuity has not ebbed or been marked for
    demolition
may break like an eggshell, and be overrun from within by the
    albumen of ruin—
their out-of-season purple not any longer hinting at something, but
    announcing it with a flourish:
the entire gorgeous, intractable realm of the forgotten,
the hieratic, the heraldic, the royal, sprung open
at the gouty foot of that anachronism
on the fringes of a kingdom that went under
at or near the downward slope of the thirteenth century. I have seen
the artesian spring of the past foam up at the foot of the castle of
    Chepstow
on a day in November, or thereabouts. I have seen a rose the size of
    a perfectly manicured crimson fingernail
alive in a winter that does not arrive, though we plunge again
    toward the solstice.

# HOMER, A.D. 1982

*For Irving Kizner and his class*
*at Hunter College*

Much having traveled in the funkier realms of Ac-
ademe, aboard a grungy elevator car,
*deus ex machina* reversed, to this ninth-floor
classroom, its windows grimy, where the noise of traffic,
πολυφλοίσβοιο-θαλάσσης-like, is chronic,
we've seen since February the stupendous candor
of the *Iliad* pour in, and for an hour and a
quarter at the core the great pulse was dactylic.

We've seen the clash, from those great halls, of light and dark,
the sullen campfires of a brooded-over choler,
Odysseus, rising, sway his peers with storms of logic,
the spurned priest of Apollo shrink along the shore,
and Hector's baby, shadowed by the plumes of war
as we are, pull back from his own father with a shriek.

# V

## WRITTEN IN WATER

# THE HICKORY GROVE

Flint-skinned, bone-hued
loot from the till of fall—
its draperies all a heap,
the latch left open—
you'll need a hammer
and a brace of nutpicks
to get at the meat of
these obdurate nuggets,

clench-kin to the KEEP OUT
that drives home what matters
is whose woods these are:
a category of autonomy
ignored by squirrels, nor
can the shambling seasons
be neatened and shut into
watertight compartments

such as memory, that burrower,
will undermine with awe,
out there in the bare-
boled, frost-bitten-eared,
enormous silences of winter:
or, alarmingly, the ramrod
shagbarks stirred, up over-
head, into one green-gold

churn of things opening and
unfolding—leaf clusters big
as wheatsheaves cascading
out of casqued sheathings
too extravagant to figure
as a source of income—the
inner burnish of all that
scrap satin such as is un-

amenable to the hard arts
of bronze, of mining and
smelting—or of pouring
an ingot of metaphor so
dazzling, some day some
critic, come round to see
these woods, will post a
sign that says PROPRIETOR.

# LOSING TRACK OF LANGUAGE

The train leaps toward Italy, the French Riviera
falls away in the dark, the rails sing dimeter
shifting to trimeter, a galopade to a galliard.
We sit wedged among strangers; whatever
we once knew (it was never much) of each other
falls away with the landscape. Words
fall away, we trade instead in flirting
and cigarettes; we're all rapport with strangers.
The one with the yellow forelock that keeps falling
and being shaken back again, syncopating
the dimeter-trimeter, galopade-into-galliard,
is, it seems, Italian—recently a pilgrim
to the Vaucluse, where Petrarca,
to the noise of waterfalls, measured out
his strict stanzas, little rooms
for turmoil to grow lucid in, for
change to put on more durable
leaves of bronze, a scapular of marble.

A splutter of pleasure at hearing the name
is all he needs, and he's off
like a racehorse at the Palio—plunging
unbridled into recited cadenzas, three-beat
lines interleaving a liquid pentameter.
What are words? They fall away into the fleeing
dark of the French Riviera, as once a shower
of bloom, *una pioggia di fior*, descended
into the lap of the Trecento: her hair
all gold and pearl, the grass still warm
as when she sat there, six centuries
gone by; that squandered heartbeat
(the black plague took her, young) now
fossilized as bronze, as carved laurel.

Whatever is left of her is language;
and what is language but breath, leaves,
petals fallen or in the act of falling, pollen
of turmoil that sifts through the fingers?

—*E conosce* (I ask it to keep the torrent
of words from ending, to keep anything
from ending, ever) *anche Sappho?* Yes,
he knows, he will oblige. The limpid pentameter
gives way to something harsher: diphthongs
condense, take on an edge of bronze. Though
I don't understand a word, what are words? Do these
concern one Timas, led before she was married
(or so one leaf of what's left would have it)
to the dark bedroom of Persephone, for so long
nowhere at home, either here or there, forever
returning and falling back again
into the dark of these ten thousand years?
The train leaps toward Italy; words fall away
through the dark into the dark bedroom
of everything left behind, the unendingness
of things lost track of—of who, of where—
where I'm losing track of language.

# WRITTEN IN WATER

From a woman's dream of being,
at her age, still deemed desirable,
preserved—the quivering reliquary
of the dew of decades snared
among the fernery—till morning,

to wake in winter to this antic
glare—the Snow Queen's frore
boudoir, the numbed orthography
of being seen, its milkweed
smithereens turned every which way—

is still to listen for the seep
within the crypt, the mirror-
drip of stalactites, blind milk
of perpetuity whose only witness
is the viewless salamander.

# A CURE AT PORLOCK

For whatever did it—the cider
at the Ship Inn, where the crowd
from the bar that night had overflowed
singing into Southey's Corner, or

an early warning of appendicitis—
the remedy the chemist in the High Street
purveyed was still a dose of kaopectate
in morphine—the bane and the afflatus

of S.T.C. when Alph, the sacred river,
surfaced briefly in the unlikely
vicinity of Baker Farm, and as quickly
sank again, routed forever by the visitor

whose business, intent and disposition—
whether ill or well is just as immaterial—
long ago sunk Lethewards, a particle
of the unbottled ultimate solution.

I drank my dose, and after an afternoon
prostrate, between heaves, on the
coldly purgatorial tiles of the W.C.,
found it elysium simply to recline,

sipping flat ginger beer as though it were
honeydew, in that billowy bed,
under pink chenille, hearing you read
*The Mystery of Edwin Drood*! For whether

the opium was worth it for John Jasper,
from finding being with you, even sick
at Porlock, a rosily addictive picnic,
I left less likely ever to recover.

Some sort of road does go up there,
they'll tell you, but unless you're
exceptionally good at maps, it's better

to go by the public footpath, rocks
and all—tree-root-contorted hummocks,
the rhododendron-filtered lilt of brooks

you never see until the footbridge,
brown water gabbling a liquid passage
underneath, and then there's the church

you've come to look at—its valley tucked
fast against a steep slope cassocked
in a murk of oaks, an apron pocket-

ful of sun. The church is very old and tiny,
surplices are laid out for next Sunday,
and the starch-smooth interior cube's as though

a whitewashed sea chapel had been lifted
up here (having been deftly introverted)
from the glare of Mýkonos. Nothing could,

though, be more un-Greek than the choir
stalls' gnarled wood-sorrel quatre-
foils—as English as to be famished for

a cup of tea. Which, as you'll have heard,
there's a lady hereabouts who can provide.
Asked, one of two men studying the underside

of a stalled car just where the road dwindles
to its dead end, says, "Well, there's Mrs.
Cook. She's deaf. Don't know if she's

there. Better knock loud"—with a gesture
toward the slope above the church tower:
a chimneyed cottage of a stone the color,

approximately, of a Cox's orange pippin,
a twirl of smoke above a steep small garden,
moss roses, gooseberry bushes, a carillon

of fuchsia trees, the gate open and then
a flight of flagstones, the door open
too, as though unaware one might walk in

and claim, on having crossed the threshold,
merely by the walking in, the unguarded
mysteries of an entire existence. Elated

almost to the brink of fear—how can
the act of entering not alter, and ruin
in altering, what one loves for having been

until this instant wholly uninfected
by oneself?—you pause, and at the threshold
of possession, you observe the sacred

coal fire on the grate, the elbowed
stovepipe, the meal dish and the bed
of a household animal; the sideboard

in the adjoining room, a reredos
of snapshots, postcards, mementos
from all over, the unself-conscious

showpiece of a lifetime that must
have—otherwise why, as you paused
just now, that tremor of an unforced

happiness?—been happy. She appears,
small, quick but unhurried. There's
a hearing aid under the wreathed hair's

bright blond gone hay-color. Yes, she can
give you tea. Since the day's fine,
will you have it here in the garden?

She lays it all out on a tablecloth,
brings biscuits and a book to autograph,
as visitors coming up by the footpath

have been doing all these years—people from
all over, depositing an unwitting perfume
of far climates along with the humdrum

"Thanx for the nice cuppa." You venture
that the church down there made you, for
a minute, think of Greece. From her

vague nod you see she hasn't followed.
The church, you say again—it's splendid.
Now she does. She tells you she was married

in it back in 1914, has lived here, in this
same cottage, ever since. Her husband's
just now ill and in hospital. No one knows

exactly what the matter was. "He's better?"
"I hope he is"—said with such composure
you're relieved, as though one might be sure

the bourn of age would prove on opening
to have inurned the blessedness of dying—
only not yet, Lord, it takes some growing

[ 97 ]

into, still. Time meanwhile to admire
the fuchsia trees, a memento (minus their
attendant hummingbirds) of the steep sea air,

the sun and fog of northern California.
She nods, with no surprise. "A lady
here who comes from California told me

it was very like. She came here for a
visit, and stayed on. She has the pottery
up there"—deferring to a building of the

same apple-colored stone, but surer
of its tone, in being new, than either
this cottage, with its sacred spire

of coal smoke, or the whitewash-walled
landmark down below. "But"—lest you should,
at this intelligence, rush up only to find

no one—"she's not there now." You have
just now not the least wish to think of
pots, or anything that might be craf-

ted in a day and given to a kiln to harden—
that oven smelling of no substance so in-
dispensable as home-made bread. To go in

for pots—to be so earthbound and so
fired-up at once—seems somehow crazy:
to be forever whacking at the clay,

forever trying out its character
with switches of local weeds, forever
making things whose function's either

merely to contain some other thing,
coffinlike, or to stand idle, wearing
the smirk of one content with being

well turned out, a calculated object.
No. No object. Better a process. No, not
that either. No process but the unshaped

accretion, the watershed, the accidental
bloom that won't survive the kiln—
being, totally untainted by the will:

only the doing without making so very
much of what one does will do—with no
particular design for giving shape to any-

thing at all, even the outlines of one's
own experience: asking for no consequence
other than those decades of sentiments

in the pages of a guest book: the whole
of what at last is no more durable
than crumbling soil, the common, friable,

finally intangible, that may come up again
as gooseberries or go down drowning un-
der the sound of brooks. Just now, one

might be tempted to drop everything, to
settle into an acquaintance with the clay,
and so put down one's roots here like the lady

from California. "Here I am!" A young
woman—or possibly one not young,
merely vivid and lissome—is rushing

up, is leaving, in leaning, a flying kiss
above the cheek and the wreathed hair of Mrs.
Cook. That, Mrs. Cook says as she vanishes,

is the lady who has the pottery.
The world is full of mystery.
A creature half California poppy,

half hummingbird, could hardly come from
any other place. But pots? Perhaps
her husband (if she has one) or some
        minion makes them.

# LET THE AIR CIRCULATE

                    spaces between
            archetypal openings        the aperture
    seen through binoculars        carved by the lone boatman's
        arm athwart the tiller        the schooner's traveling
        house of air   split like a nutshell   or a bivalve's domicile
            jalousies     belfries     cupolas     floor-through
    apartments      let the air circulate        spaces between (sixteen
            floors up and still rising)        scaffolded pourers
    of reinforced concrete       by the motorized      wheelbarrowful
        silhouetted   (a hardhatted frieze)   make of them
                something unwittingly classical


                    clamdiggers
        wading mudflats                        bending in attitudes
    older than            the names of anything            spaces between
            things looked at    or unlooked at    beatitudes
            of the unaware they're    being looked at
    eiders flying        straight as a die        to wherever they're going
        triglyph and metope        of air        let the light pass
        let the air circulate            let there be intervals
            for moving            apart            for
                    coming back together


                    the antipodal
            the antiphonal            the gradual
        the totally unexpected        the counted on        as infallible
            the look of        from a particular        window
                    an island        in profile
            the fish-spine        silhouette        of a particular
        spruce    intersecting at nightfall    the unaltering interval
            of 'Tit Manan light    opening up    folding into
                itself    fading    brightening    an orbiting
                    sidereal buttercup

# NOTES

### *"The August Darks"*

"Herring prefer to come inshore on the dark of the moon," according to a report published in the *Ellsworth* [Maine] *American* for August 5, 1982, and headlined "The August Darks."

From *Middlemarch*, by George Eliot, Book II, Chapter 20: "If we had a keen vision and feeling of all ordinary human life, it would be like hearing the grass grow and the squirrel's heart beat, and we should die of that roar which lies on the other side of silence. As it is, the quickest of us walk about well wadded with stupidity."

### *"Low Tide at Schoodic"*

From *The Geology of Acadia National Park* by Carlton A. Chapman (Chatham Press, 1970): "An outstanding feature of Schoodic Point is the abundance of dark-colored basaltic dikes, which range up to many yards in width and run through the granite ledges. . . . About 450 million years ago . . . the sea covered a large part of New England and widespread layers of sand, silt, and mud were accumulating upon its floor. . . . After these . . . had accumulated to a total thickness of hundreds and perhaps even thousands of feet, the southeastern portion of Maine became an unstable region and crustal movement (diastrophism) set in. . . . Hot fluid, similar to the black lava of Hawaii's volcanoes, was squeezed upward and sought the easiest means of access to the stratified rocks above. Zones of weakness, such as large fractures in the crustal rocks, permitted rapid influx of the magma. . . ."

From *The Audubon Society Field Guide to North American Seashore Creatures* by Norman A. Meinkoth (Alfred A. Knopf, 1981): "The white barnacles seen at low tide covering rocks and pilings on the seacoast are sedentary crustaceans. They secrete limy shells composed of many interlocking plates, often with a trapdoor opening at the top that can be closed for protection."

### *"Cloudberry Summer"*

On barnacles, from *A Field Guide to the Atlantic Seashore* by Kenneth L. Gosner (Houghton Mifflin, Boston, 1978): "The adult animal has been described as shrimplike and glued down by the top of its head. When covered with water, the barnacle rhythmically opens and closes its trapdoors to extend the six pairs of feathery *cirri* like a small hand, grasping blindly for any planktonic or detrital morsels adrift in the water."

On lemmings, from *The Hunting Animal* by Franklin Russell (Harper & Row, New York, 1983), p. 209: "Family after identical family came out of the earth, one new generation every thirteen or fourteen days. A little more than one hundred days of breeding spewed out seven hundred and fifty descendants from one family. Children were breeding, and grandchildren, and very soon, great-grandchildren approached each other to mate. . . . After the plowing, the lemmings polluted. What they did not eat down to the roots, which was almost everything, they despoiled with their sewage, changing the flowering earth into a wasteland. This sent them into hasty movement, urgent mini-migrations. But horde met horde. Finally, when all was eaten out for miles, the hordes combined and began mass movements, anywhere, everywhere, nowhere. It was not true that they committed suicide by jumping into the sea. They had to leave the land because they had eaten it bare."

## "A Curfew"

On Alfred Russel Wallace, from *Darwin and the Mysterious Mr. X* by Loren Eiseley (E. P. Dutton, New York, 1979), pp. 25–26: "During the early months of 1858 Wallace was living at Ternate in the Molucca Islands off the western tip of New Guinea. He was suffering severely from intermittent fever, and during one of these attacks, while he lay weak but lucid on his bed, his mind began to revolve upon the 'species problem' which had fascinated him. . . . 'Something,' he says, 'brought to my recollection Malthus's *Principle of Population* which I had read about twelve years before.' In a lightning flash of insight, it occurred to the feverish naturalist that Malthus's checks to human increase—accident, disease, war, and famine—must, in similar or analogous ways, operate in the natural world as well. 'Vaguely thinking over the enormous and constant destruction which this implied, it occurred to me,' he tells us, 'to ask the question, "Why do some die and some live?" ' The answer, Wallace felt, was clear: the best fitted live. 'From the effects of disease the most healthy escaped; from the enemies the strongest, the swiftest, or the most cunning; from famine, the best hunters. . . . Considering the amount of individual variation that my experience as a collector had shown me to exist, then it followed that all the changes necessary for the adaptation of the species to the changing conditions would be brought about; and as great changes in the environment are always slow, there would be ample time for the change to be effected by the survival of the best fitted in every generation.' "

On Democritus, from *The Worlds of the Early Greek Philosophers* by J. B. Wilbur and H. J. Allen (Prometheus Books, Buffalo, New York, 1979), pp. 183, 187: "Democritus was called the Laughing Philosopher by Cicero and Horace, presumably because of his reaction to human folly. . . . For Leucippus and Democritus, . . . everything must be explained in terms of movements in a void of material atoms governed by necessity. . . ."

On Heraclitus, from the same source, pp. 66, 67: "Fundamental to Heraclitus' ontology is his notion of the pervasiveness of change. . . . The theme of the flowing river epitomizes Heraclitus' approach to change—so much so that he has been called 'the river philosopher.' (Frg. 91, 1st part) 'It is not possible to step twice into the same river. . . .' "

## "Urn-Burial and the Butterfly Migration"

From *Hydriotaphia*, by Sir Thomas Browne, Chapter 1: "Time hath endless rarities, and shows of all varieties; which reveals old things in heaven, makes new discoveries in earth, and even earth it self a discovery. That great antiquity *America* lay buried for thousands of years; and a large part of the earth is still in the Urne unto us. . . . Many have taken voluminous pains to determine the state of the soul upon disunion; but men have been most phantasticall in the singular contrivances of their corporall dissolution: whilest the sobrest Nations have rested in two wayes, of simple inhumation and burning. . . . Some being of the opinion of *Thales*, that water was the originall of all things, thought it most equall to submit unto the principle of putrefaction, and conclude in a moist relentment. Others conceived it most natural to end in fire, as due unto the master principle in the composition, according to the doctrine of Heraclitus. . . . the old Heroes in *Homer* dreaded nothing more than water or drowning; probably upon the old opinion of the fiery substance of the soul. . . ." From Chapter 3 of the same work: "How the bulk of a man should sink into so few pounds of bones and ashes, may seem strange unto any who considers not its constitution, and how slender a masse will remain upon an open and urging fire of the carnall composition. Even bones themselves reduced into ashes, do abate a notable proportion. And consisting much of a volatile salt, when that is fired out, make a light kind of cinders. Although their bulk be disproportionable to their weight, when the heavy principle of Salt is fired out and the Earth almost only remaineth. . . ."

MONARCH. . . . 4. a species of large, migrating butterfly of North America, having reddish-brown, black-edged wings: the larvae feed on milkweed. *Webster's New Universal Unabridged Dictionary.*

### "Voyages: A Homage to John Keats"

In the summer and early fall of 1816, John Keats spent two months at the seaside resort of Margate, on the English Channel. It was here that he saw the ocean for the first time. He was not quite twenty-one, and had only recently begun to think of himself as a poet. Not long after his return to London he stayed up all one night reading aloud with a friend from George Chapman's translation of the *Odyssey*, and wrote his now famous sonnet, "On First Looking into Chapman's Homer." In the spring of the following year he was back at Margate, reading Shakespeare and working on a long poem of his own. On May 10, 1817, he wrote to his friend B. R. Haydon, "I have been in such a state of Mind as to read over my Lines and hate them. I am 'one that gathers Samphire dreadful trade' the cliff of Poesy towers above me. . . ."—a reference to Act IV, Scene 6 of *King Lear*:

> Come, sir; here is the place: stand still. How fearful
> And dizzy 'tis to cast one's eyes so low!

The crows and choughs that wing the midway air
Show scarce so gross as beetles; half way down
Hangs one that gathers samphire, dreadful trade!

(Samphire or glasswort is a fleshy seaside herb that is at least better to eat than nothing.) In that scene Gloucester, who has been blinded for remaining loyal to King Lear, is being led through the countryside near Dover, which is not many miles down the coast from Margate itself—a circumstance that must have added to its effect on Keats's own imagination. The powerful way in which literature can become a link with times and places, and with minds, otherwise remote, suggested itself to me as I read W. Jackson Bate's biography, *John Keats* (Harvard University Press, 1963). It was here that I came upon the account by a contemporary, Joseph Severn, of how Keats would pause during a walk across Hampstead Heath to watch the passage of the wind over a field of grain: "The sea, or thought-compelling images of the sea, always seemed to restore him to a happy calm." The idea of John Keats pausing to take in a sight that had been familiar to me since childhood connected itself in turn with images of the ocean in the work of Whitman and Hart Crane. For connecting Keats with Osip Mandelstam, there is at any rate the authority of Nadezhda Mandelstam's observation (in *Mozart and Salieri*, p. 23): "Akhmatova used to say that Keats almost physiologically reminded her of Mandelstam." And that Wallace Stevens might also be intimately linked with Keats was suggested to me by an essay of Helen Vendler, "Stevens and Keats' 'To Autumn'" (in *Part of Nature, Part of Us*, Harvard University Press, 1980), for which I wish here to acknowledge my enormous indebtedness.

The lines quoted in the epigraph are from an untitled octet, as translated by David McDuff in *Selected Poems of Osip Mandelstam* (Farrar, Straus and Giroux, 1975; p. 129). Other poems paraphrased or alluded to in the concluding poem of the sequence may be found on pp. 11, 37, 111, 123, and 163 of the same volume.

In the final poem of the sequence, the third and fourth stanzas draw upon "Porphyro in Akron" from *The Complete Poems and Selected Letters and Prose of Hart Crane*, edited by Brom Weber (Anchor Books, New York, 1966), pp. 144–46, which concludes:

But look up, Porphyro,—your toes
Are ridiculously tapping
The spindles at the foot of the bed.

The stars are drowned in a slow rain,
And a hash of noises is slung up from the street.
You ought, really, to try to sleep,
Even though, in this town, poetry's a
Bedroom occupation.

## "The Reedbeds of the Hackensack"

REED, n. . . . . 1. any of various tall, broad-leaved, related grasses with jointed, hollow stems which grow along the banks of streams . . . especially *Phragmites communis*, the common reed. This is the largest of all the grasses of northern climates, and one of the most universally diffused. It is used for thatching, for protecting embankments, for roofing, etc. 2. a mass of these, growing or dried. 3. a rustic musical instrument made from a hollow stem or stalk and played by blowing through it: used as the symbol of pastoral poetry. *Webster's New Universal Unabridged Dictionary*.

From *Return to the Marshes: Life with the Marsh Arabs of Iraq* by Gavin Young (Collins, London, 1977), pp. 16, 34: ". . . often, out of some apparently deserted reed-jungle, a full-throated human voice soared into the silence—a young Marsh Arab singing a love-song as he harvested the rushes. . . . In that great solitude, where the men of Ur once poled their canoes and where 'in the beginning,' according to Sumerian legend, Marduk, the great God, built a reed platform on the surface of the waters and thus created the world, the effect is one of unquenchable and universal yearning. . . . The numerous Sumerian city-states . . . were large and sophisticated settlements consisting of suburbs, satellite towns, gardens and orchards. . . . In the cities on the fringe of the giant reed-beds, writing was born (about 3000 B.C.) and developed, at first in the form of pictographs, simple drawings scratched on clay with reed stalks. . . ."

Allusions to and/or borrowings from the poems of William Carlos Williams, Dante, Milton, Keats, and Shakespeare will be noted in this poem, which may be regarded as a last-ditch effort to associate the landscape familiarly known as the Jersey Meadows with the tradition of elegiac poetry.

## "Real Estate"

"Urban Relocation (Not A/ Governmental Agency)": A private firm retained by the owners of tenement buildings intended for demolition but still inhabited, Urban Relocation had chosen a name of such bureaucratic portentousness that it was obliged to distinguish itself in this fashion.

## "Homer, A.D. 1982"

The descriptive epithet πολυφλοίσβοιο-θαλάσσης (variously translated as "loud-roaring," "heavy-thundering," or simply "murmuring" and pronounced *poluphloísboio-thalássēs*) recurs throughout the *Iliad*; its first appearance is in line 34 of the first book, in which the reader sees "the spurned priest of Apollo shrink along the shore." The surprising eloquence of Odysseus is described in lines 216–23 of the third book, and the scene in which the infant Astyanax is frightened by the sight of his father Hector in the horsehair-plumed war helmet he wore as he said goodbye to his family occurs in Book 6, lines 466–70.

## "Losing Track of Language"

The Canzone of Petrarch referred to in the second stanza is the one beginning, "Chiare, fresche e dolci aque." The poem of Sappho referred to in the concluding stanza is Number 20 in *Sappho: A New Translation* by Mary Barnard (University of California Press, Berkeley and Los Angeles, 1958).

### "A Cure at Porlock"

"In the summer of the year 1797, the Author, then in ill health, had retired to a lonely farm-house between Porlock and Linton, on the Exmoor confines of Somerset and Devonshire. In consequence of a slight indisposition, an anodyne had been prescribed, from the effect of which he fell asleep in his chair. . . . The Author continued for about three hours in a profound sleep, at least of the external senses, during which time he has the most vivid confidence that he could not have composed less than from two to three hundred lines. . . . On waking he appeared to himself to have a distinct recollection of the whole, and taking his pen, ink, and paper, instantly and eagerly wrote down the lines that are here preserved. At this moment he was unfortunately called out by a person on business from Porlock, and detained by him above an hour, and on his return to his room, found . . . that . . . with the exception of some eight or ten scattered lines and images, all the rest had been passed away like the images on the surface of a stream into which a stone had been cast. . . ." This is Samuel Taylor Coleridge's account, written some years later, of the composition of "Kubla Khan." The anodyne he mentions was presumably a form of opium, to which he was addicted for much of his adult life. The ravages of such addiction, as embodied in the character of John Jasper, form a major theme of Dickens's unfinished last novel, *The Mystery of Edwin Drood*.